A Day in the Life: Polar Animals

Reindeer

Katie Marsico

Heinemann Library
Chicago, Illinois

www.capstonepub.com
Visit our website to find out
more information about
Heinemann-Raintree books.

To order:
☎ Phone 800-747-4992
💻 Visit www.capstonepub.com
   to browse our catalog and order online.

© 2012 Heinemann Library
an imprint of Capstone Global Library, LLC
Chicago, Illinois

Edited by Rebecca Rissman, Daniel Nunn, and
Sian Smith
Designed by Joanna Hinton-Malivoire
Picture research by Hannah Taylor
Originated by Capstone Global Library Ltd
Printed in the United States of America in
Eau Claire, Wisconsin

110315
009323RP

Library of Congress Cataloging-in-Publication Data

Marsico, Katie, 1980-
  Reindeer / Katie Marsico.—1st ed.
    p. cm.—(A day in the life: polar animals)
  Includes bibliographical references and index.
  ISBN 978-1-4329-5330-0 (hb)
  ISBN 978-1-4329-5337-9 (pb)
  1. Reindeer—Juvenile literature. I. Title.
  QL737.U55M2966 2012
    599.65'8—dc22   2010050014

Acknowledgments

We would like to thank the following for permission to
reproduce photographs: Corbis pp. 7 (Frank Krahmer),
8, 23c (Christophe Boisvieux), 13 (Layne Kennedy); FLPA
pp. 5, 23b (Mark Newman), 10 (Minden Pictures/Colin
Monteath), 11, 23a (Minden Pictures/ Michio Hoshino),
14 (imagebroker/Horst Jegen), 17 (Minden Pictures/
Michio Hoshino), 20 (Minden Pictures/ Michio Hoshino);
Photolibrary pp. 4 (imagebroker/ Michael Krabs), 6 (age
fotostock/ Mark Hamblin), 15, 23f (Imagebroker RF), 16
(Oxford Scientific/Daniel J. Cox), 19 (Imagebroker RF),
21, 23e (Imagebroker RF), 22 (Oxford Scientific/ Mark
Hamblin); Shutterstock pp. 9 (© Roman Krochuk), 12, 23d
(© pzAxe), 18 (© Witold Kaszkin).

Cover photograph of a reindeer (Rangifer tarandus) in
snow reproduced with permission of Alamy Images (©
WILDLIFE GmbH). Back cover photographs reproduced
with permission of Shutterstock: lichen (© pzAxe), antlers
(© Witold Kaszkin).

The publisher would like to thank Michael Bright for his
assistance in the preparation of this book.

Every effort has been made to contact copyright holders
of material reproduced in this book. Any omissions will
be rectified in subsequent printings if notice is given to the
publisher.

Disclaimer

Contents

Some words are shown in bold, **like this**.
You can find them in the glossary on page 23.

What Is a Reindeer?

A reindeer is a large **mammal** that often lives in snowy areas.

All mammals have some hair on their bodies and feed their babies milk.

antlers

Reindeer have **antlers** on their heads.

Antlers are hard body parts that are shaped like tree branches.

What Do Reindeer Look Like?

hooves

Reindeer have wide hooves that help them to walk on snow and dig for food.

Reindeer usually have fur that is a blend of gray and brown.

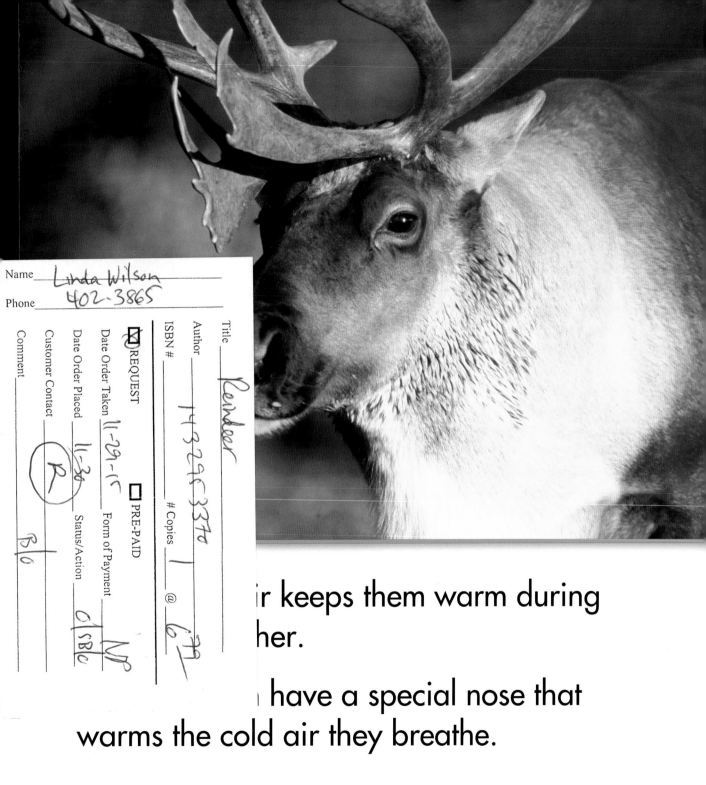

ir keeps them warm during
her.

have a special nose that
warms the cold air they breathe.

Where Do Reindeer Live?

Arctic

Reindeer live in a part of the world called the **Arctic**.

In the Arctic it is light all day and all night for part of the summer.

In the Arctic it is dark all day and all night for part of the winter.

The Arctic is one of the coldest and windiest places in the world!

What Do Reindeer Do in the Day?

Reindeer are usually most **active** during the day.

They start their day by waking up and looking for food.

Reindeer travel long distances each year to search for food.

They often walk across frozen ground and swim through icy waters.

What Do Reindeer Eat?

lichen

Reindeer eat **lichen** that grows beneath the snow.

There are many different types of lichen.

Reindeer use their hooves to uncover lichen.

They also eat whatever grasses and leaves they can find during warmer months.

What Hunts Reindeer?

golden eagle

Gray wolves, polar bears, and brown bears hunt reindeer.

Golden eagles sometimes attack young reindeer.

wolverine

Wolverines attack reindeer too.

People also hunt reindeer for their meat and **antlers**.

Do Reindeer Live in Groups?

Reindeer live in groups called herds.

There can be dozens to hundreds of reindeer in a herd.

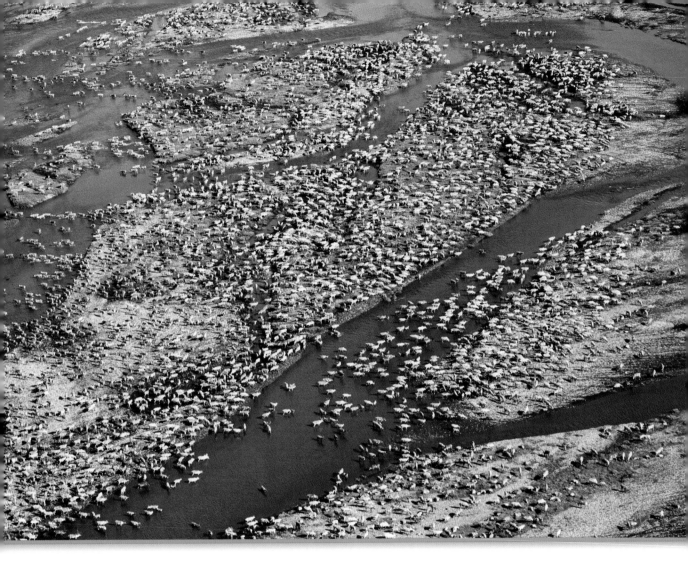

When reindeer travel long distances, small herds often join together to form large groups.

There are sometimes hundreds of thousands of animals in these herds!

What Do Reindeer Do at Night?

Reindeer may spend part of the night looking for food.

They often do this in the summer, when it is light all day and all night.

Reindeer rest more during the night or just after feeding.

Sometimes they lie down to sleep, but they can also sleep standing up.

What Are Baby Reindeer Like?

baby

Mother reindeer give birth to a single baby once a year.

Babies are often born in the morning and start traveling with the herd within hours.

A baby reindeer is called a calf.

After about three or four months the calf grows **antlers** and learns to survive without its mother.

Reindeer Body Map

antlers

fur

nose

hooves

Glossary

 **active** busy doing lots of things

 **antlers** hard body parts that grow from a reindeer's head

 **Arctic** area surrounding the North Pole. It is very cold in the Arctic.

 **lichen** plants that look like moss and that have no leaves, stem, or roots

 **mammal** animal that feeds its babies milk. All mammals have some hair or fur on their bodies.

 **wolverines** strong weasels known for their fierce hunting skills

Find Out More

Websites

kids.nationalgeographic.com/kids/animals/creaturefeature/caribou/
In some places reindeer are also called caribou. Watch a video and find out more about them on this Website.

www.biokids.umich.edu/critters/Rangifer_tarandus/
Find out all about reindeer on this BioKids Website.

Index